Rhythmic Gymnastics

By: Sunflower Design Publishing

Copyright © 2019

All rights reserved.

ISBN-13:9781797725888

Journaling is an excellent way to reinforce learning, stay organized, and to express yourself. Jot down your feelings, techniques you need to work on, warm-up routines, performance notes, or competition feedback. This journal is for you!

This journal includes sections on:

Lined pages for Routines or General/Competition Notes

Organizational Pages: Performance (Gym or Competition), Choreographer/Coach, Dance Style, Music Selection, Routine Notes, Technique, & Costume Notes

17 Short Term & 3 Long Term Goal Pages

Dedication Page: This page is to reflect upon the work documented in this journal and to aspire towards the future.

Enjoy!

Performance:

_____

_____

Choreographer/Coach:

_____

_____

Dance Style:

_____

_____

Music Selection:

_____

_____

_____

Routine Notes:

_____

_____

_____

_____

_____

_____

_____

_____

_____

Technique Notes:

_____

_____

_____

_____

_____

_____

_____

_____

Costume Notes:

_____

_____

_____

_____

_____

_____

_____

Goal #1

My goal is to…

_____

_____

_____

_____

_____

I will achieve this goal by:

_____

_____

_____

My Reward is:

_____

_____

_____

_____

Performance:

_____

_____

Choreographer/Coach:

_____

_____

Dance Style:

_____

_____

Music Selection:

_____

_____

_____

Routine Notes:

_____

_____

_____

_____

_____

_____

_____

_____

_____

Technique Notes:

_____

_____

_____

_____

_____

_____

_____

_____

Costume Notes:

_____

_____

_____

_____

_____

_____

_____

_____

Goal #2

My goal is to…

_____

_____

_____

_____

_____

_____

I will achieve this goal by:

_____

_____

_____

My Reward is:

_____

_____

_____

_____

Performance:

_____

_____

Choreographer/Coach:

_____

_____

Dance Style:

_____

_____

Music Selection:

_____

_____

_____

Routine Notes:

_____

_____

_____

_____

_____

_____

_____

_____

_____

Technique Notes:

_____

_____

_____

_____

_____

_____

_____

Costume Notes:

_____

_____

_____

_____

_____

_____

_____

Goal #3

My goal is to…

_____

_____

_____

_____

_____

_____

I will achieve this goal by:

_____

_____

_____

My Reward is:

_____

_____

_____

_____

_____

Performance:

Choreographer/Coach:

Dance Style:

Music Selection:

Routine Notes:

Technique Notes:

_____

_____

_____

_____

_____

_____

_____

Costume Notes:

_____

_____

_____

_____

_____

_____

_____

Goal #4

My goal is to…

_____

_____

_____

_____

_____

_____

I will achieve this goal by:

_____

_____

_____

My Reward is:

_____

_____

_____

_____

Performance:

_____

_____

Choreographer/Coach:

_____

_____

Dance Style:

_____

_____

Music Selection:

_____

_____

_____

Routine Notes:

_____

_____

_____

_____

_____

_____

_____

_____

_____

Technique Notes:

_____

_____

_____

_____

_____

_____

_____

_____

_____

Costume Notes:

_____

_____

_____

_____

_____

_____

_____

_____

Goal #5

My goal is to...

_____

_____

_____

_____

_____

_____

_____

I will achieve this goal by:

_____

_____

_____

_____

My Reward is:

_____

_____

_____

_____

_____

Performance:

_____

_____

Choreographer/Coach:

_____

_____

Dance Style:

_____

_____

Music Selection:

_____

_____

Routine Notes:

_____

_____

_____

_____

_____

_____

_____

_____

_____

_____

Technique Notes:

_____

_____

_____

_____

_____

_____

_____

_____

Costume Notes:

_____

_____

_____

_____

_____

_____

_____

_____

Goal #6

My goal is to…

_____

_____

_____

_____

_____

_____

I will achieve this goal by:

_____

_____

_____

My Reward is:

_____

_____

_____

_____

Performance:

_____

_____

Choreographer/Coach:

_____

_____

Dance Style:

_____

_____

Music Selection:

_____

_____

_____

Routine Notes:

_____

_____

_____

_____

_____

_____

_____

_____

_____

_____

Technique Notes:

_____

_____

_____

_____

_____

_____

_____

_____

Costume Notes:

_____

_____

_____

_____

_____

_____

_____

_____

Goal #7

My goal is to…

_____

_____

_____

_____

_____

_____

_____

I will achieve this goal by:

_____

_____

_____

_____

My Reward is:

_____

_____

_____

_____

_____

Performance:

_____

_____

Choreographer/Coach:

_____

_____

Dance Style:

_____

_____

Music Selection:

_____

_____

_____

Routine Notes:

_____

_____

_____

_____

_____

_____

_____

_____

_____

_____

Technique Notes:

_____

_____

_____

_____

_____

_____

_____

_____

_____

Costume Notes:

_____

_____

_____

_____

_____

_____

_____

_____

Goal #8

My goal is to…

_____

_____

_____

_____

_____

_____

_____

I will achieve this goal by:

_____

_____

_____

My Reward is:

_____

_____

_____

_____

_____

Performance:

_____

Choreographer/Coach:

_____

Dance Style:

_____

Music Selection:

_____

_____

Routine Notes:

_____

_____

_____

_____

_____

_____

_____

_____

_____

_____

Technique Notes:

_____

_____

_____

_____

_____

_____

_____

_____

_____

Costume Notes:

_____

_____

_____

_____

_____

_____

_____

_____

_____

Goal #9

My goal is to…

_____

_____

_____

_____

_____

_____

I will achieve this goal by:

_____

_____

_____

My Reward is:

_____

_____

_____

_____

Performance:

_____

_____

Choreographer/Coach:

_____

_____

Dance Style:

_____

_____

Music Selection:

_____

_____

_____

Routine Notes:

_____

_____

_____

_____

_____

_____

_____

_____

_____

_____

Technique Notes:

_____

_____

_____

_____

_____

_____

_____

_____

_____

_____

Costume Notes:

_____

_____

_____

_____

_____

Goal #10

My goal is to…

_____

_____

_____

_____

_____

I will achieve this goal by:

_____

_____

_____

_____

_____

My Reward is:

_____

_____

_____

_____

_____

_____

_____

_____

Performance:

_____

_____

Choreographer/Coach:

_____

_____

Dance Style:

_____

_____

Music Selection:

_____

_____

_____

Routine Notes:

_____

_____

_____

_____

_____

_____

_____

_____

_____

_____

Technique Notes:

_____

_____

_____

_____

_____

_____

_____

_____

Costume Notes:

_____

_____

_____

_____

_____

_____

_____

Goal #11

My Goal is to…

_____

_____

_____

_____

_____

_____

I will achieve this goal by:

_____

_____

_____

_____

My Reward is:

_____

_____

_____

_____

_____

_____

Performance:

_____

Choreographer/Coach:

_____

Dance Style:

_____

Music Selection:

_____

_____

Routine Notes:

_____

_____

_____

_____

_____

_____

_____

_____

Technique Notes:

_____

_____

_____

_____

_____

_____

_____

_____

Costume Notes:

_____

_____

_____

_____

_____

_____

_____

_____

Goal #12

My goal is to…

_____

_____

_____

_____

_____

_____

_____

I will achieve this goal by:

_____

_____

_____

My Reward is:

_____

_____

_____

_____

_____

Performance:

_____

Choreographer/Coach:

_____

Dance Style:

_____

Music Selection:

_____

_____

Routine Notes:

_____

_____

_____

_____

_____

_____

_____

_____

Technique Notes:

_____

_____

_____

_____

_____

_____

_____

_____

Costume Notes:

_____

_____

_____

_____

_____

_____

_____

Goal #13

My goal is to…

_____

_____

_____

_____

_____

_____

I will achieve this goal by:

_____

_____

_____

My Reward is:

_____

_____

_____

_____

_____

_____

Performance:

_____

_____

Choreographer/Coach:

_____

_____

Dance Style:

_____

_____

Music Selection:

_____

_____

_____

Routine Notes:

_____

_____

_____

_____

_____

_____

_____

_____

_____

_____

Technique Notes:

_____

_____

_____

_____

_____

_____

_____

_____

Costume Notes:

_____

_____

_____

_____

_____

_____

_____

_____

Goal #14

My goal is to…

_____

_____

_____

_____

_____

_____

I will achieve this goal by:

_____

_____

_____

My Reward is:

_____

_____

_____

_____

Performance:

_____

_____

Choreographer/Coach:

_____

_____

Dance Style:

_____

_____

Music Selection:

_____

_____

_____

Routine Notes:

_____

_____

_____

_____

_____

_____

_____

_____

_____

_____

_____

Technique Notes:

_____

_____

_____

_____

_____

_____

_____

_____

Costume Notes:

_____

_____

_____

_____

_____

_____

_____

Goal #15

My goal is to…

_____

_____

_____

_____

_____

_____

_____

I will achieve this goal by:

_____

_____

_____

_____

My Reward is:

_____

_____

_____

_____

_____

_____

_____

Performance:

_____

_____

Choreographer/Coach

_____

_____

Dance Style:

_____

_____

Music Selection:

_____

_____

Routine Notes:

_____

_____

_____

_____

_____

_____

_____

_____

_____

_____

Technique Notes:

_____

_____

_____

_____

_____

_____

_____

_____

_____

Costume Notes:

_____

_____

_____

_____

_____

_____

_____

_____

Goal #16

My goal is to…

_____

_____

_____

_____

_____

_____

I will achieve this goal by:

_____

_____

_____

My Reward is:

_____

_____

_____

_____

_____

Performance:

_____

_____

Choreographer/Coach:

_____

_____

Dance Style:

_____

_____

Music Selection:

_____

_____

_____

Field/Routine Notes:

_____

_____

_____

_____

_____

_____

_____

_____

_____

_____

Technique Notes:

_____

_____

_____

_____

_____

_____

_____

_____

Costume Notes:

_____

_____

_____

_____

_____

_____

_____

_____

Goal #17

My goal is to…

_____

_____

_____

_____

_____

_____

_____

I will achieve this goal by:

_____

_____

_____

My Reward is:

_____

_____

_____

_____

_____

Performance:

_____

_____

Choreographer/Coach:

_____

_____

Dance Style:

_____

_____

Music Selection:

_____

_____

_____

Routine Notes:

_____

_____

_____

_____

_____

_____

_____

_____

_____

_____

Technique Notes:

_____

_____

_____

_____

_____

_____

_____

_____

Costume Notes:

_____

_____

_____

_____

_____

_____

_____

_____

Long Term Goal #18

My goal is to…

_____

_____

_____

_____

_____

_____

_____

I will achieve this goal by:

_____

_____

_____

_____

My Reward is:

_____

_____

_____

_____

_____

_____

Long Term Goal #19

My goal is to…

_____

_____

_____

_____

_____

_____

I will achieve this goal by:

_____

_____

_____

_____

My Reward is:

_____

_____

_____

_____

_____

_____

_____

Long Term Goal #20

My goal is to…

_____

_____

_____

_____

_____

_____

I will achieve this goal by:

_____

_____

_____

_____

My Reward is:

_____

_____

_____

_____

_____

_____

_____

I dedicate my work throughout this journal to…

_____

_____

_____

_____

_____

_____

_____

_____

_____

_____

_____

_____

_____

_____

_____

_____

Made in the USA
Monee, IL
24 February 2023

28646956R00083